Bonding With My Trauma

Poems to inspire, written by a survivor.

Chelsie Peck

BookLeaf Publishing

India | USA | UK

Made with ❤ on the BookLeaf Publishing Platform
www.bookleafpub.in
www.bookleafpub.com

Dedication

This book is dedicated to all of those who are surviving or have survived. This book aims to raise awareness of domestic violence and help others come to terms with life after surviving.

This book serves as a reminder that you are strong, determined and not alone.

Preface

In my early twenties I met a man who I thought one day
I would marry.
Little did I know, I would find myself in a physically and
emotionally abusive relationship that almost took
everything from me.
These poems were my way of expressing myself after
being silent for so long.
This book aims to provide an awareness as well as
validate the effects of abuse.

Acknowledgements

Thank you to my friends, family and colleagues for your support during this part of my journey.
I am eternally grateful for all of your encouragement and love.
Thank you to those who have gone above and beyond trying to understand me, even on the days I didn't understand myself.
Your guidance and care is worth more than its weight in gold.

Preface

In my early twenties I met a man who I thought one day I would marry.
Little did I know, I would find myself in a physically and emotionally abusive relationship that almost took everything from me.
These poems were my way of expressing myself after being silent for so long.
This book aims to provide an awareness as well as validate the effects of abuse.

Acknowledgements

Thank you to my friends, family and colleagues for your support during this part of my journey.
I am eternally grateful for all of your encouragement and love.
Thank you to those who have gone above and beyond trying to understand me, even on the days I didn't understand myself.
Your guidance and care is worth more than its weight in gold.

1. He Loves Me

You love each part of me, both smooth and scarred,
The sides of me that life made hard.

You see my flaws, yet still you stay,
You chase the darkest doubt away.

You make me feel a calm so new,
Like storms have passed, and skies turned blue.

Your touch, a flame upon my skin,
A spark where tenderness begins.

Two souls aligned by fate's design,
A meeting written in the spine.

A love that made time lose its pace,
Two heartbeats locked in warm embrace.

You called us Yin and Yang one night,

Your shadow drawn into my light.

The good to evil you once said—
An evil untold, that sleeps in my bed.

2. A Love To Last

You make me happy, pure and free,
A love that felt how it should be.

Thoughtful gestures, soft and bright,
For all to see, your love's pure light.

It happened fast, too quick to see,
The things you'd do, what you'd do to me.

Before I could blink, you had my heart,
Telling me we'd never part.

My life before you—just a ghost,
A shadow of the life I'd lost.

You made me believe, you made me trust,
That love like ours would never rust.

But deep inside, I feel the twist,
A quiet whisper, an iron fist.

What once was bright would grow so cold,
A story of love that's yet to fold.

3. Apartment Two

I picked up our keys,
To Apartment Two,
The world our oyster,
Just me and you.

Away from my family,
Far from my friends,
It didn't matter,
Together 'til the end.

A little home,
A place to grow,
A space to watch
Our love's light flow.

You could do what you wanted,
Freedoms wide and free,
The seeds of our future,
Planted so carelessly.

But in the silence,
I feel a shift,
A change that stirs,
A crack in the rift.

The dream we built—
would start to fray,
A love once whole,
I didn't know, would fade away.

4. My First Time

The first time you struck me,
With your hands so bare,
You grabbed my legs,
And pulled on my hair.

The change in your face,
My heart skipped a beat,
The rhythm of fear,
A pounding heartbeat.

I begged and I pleaded,
In a desperate grace,
But nothing could stop
The fury you'd chase.

The furniture crooked,
Thrown all around,
The air thick with tension,
A fear I had found.

Your eyes grew wide,
A glare in your stare,
For the first time,
Your love finally bare.

5. The Sun On My Face

As I lay here,
With the sun on my face,
A new day begins,
In our hollowed space.

A mistake you made,
A scar left behind,
I lay here numb,
With a shattered mind.

Stuck in this moment,
Too tired to move,
Trapped in this home,
With nothing to prove.

The birds outside,
Sing so loud and free,
They dance in the air,
But they're not singing for me.

The sun on my face,
A brief, fleeting grace,
For a second I forgot,
The hurt in this place.

It wrapped me in warmth,
Like an old friend's embrace,
A tender reminder
Of a love I can't face.

6. Shades Of Blue

As I wake up,
I glance over to you,
Sound asleep,
A day brand new.

Rubbing my sores,
From the night before,
Remembering you,
And me on the floor.

Shades of blue,
And welts in red,
A smile still painted
On your sleepy head.
Was it my fault?
I can't even tell,
It must have been,
Under your cruel spell.

7. Denial

Anger can blind,
And words can betray,
In the heat of the moment,
He had lost his way.

I wish I could take back,
The pain that I've sown,
To mend all the pieces,
And not feel alone.

The sharpness of words,
That cut to the core,
Regret fills my heart,
As I try to restore.

The moments we lost,
To anger and pride,
I long for the peace,
That we pushed aside.

If only I knew,
How to make things right,
I'd turn back the hands
And fight through the night.

To heal all the hurt,
And rewrite our song,
To right all the wrongs,
Before they're too long.

But for now, I wait,
For time to forgive,
And hope that someday,
We'll learn how to live.

8. This Love

We went out for drinks,
Danced the night away,
But we ended it,
In anger and dismay.

You told other women,
How gorgeous they were,
While I stood by,
And watched you flirt.

You grabbed her waist,
Pulled her in tight,
While I stood there,
Invisible in the night.

I couldn't tell,
Where I'd gone wrong,
To make you forget me,
Where I once belonged.

9. Date Night

I did my makeup,
Curled my hair,
I wondered that night,
How your love would fare.

You downed your drink,
And off we went,
A date night together,
A night well spent.

Little did I know,
You'd lose control,
The colours of green, blue and red,
A mark on my soul.

The way your face shifted,
Love turned to disdain,
The mosaic on my body,
A constant, aching stain.

Your love like distemper,
The marks on my body,
Sore and tender.

10. Beautiful Hues

Hues of red, blue, and green,
The marks on my body,
From where you'd been.

Images flash,
Over and over,
Of you and your hands,
Even when sober.

My body a prism,
A canvas so strange,
With bright forest greens,
And deep ocean change.

The bruises, though painful,
Shine in their grace,
A map of my struggle,
Etched in this space.

11. Shame

This isn't my life,
It can't be,
Surely,
This isn't me.

My parents were proud,
My friends held me near,
But in the silence,
I disappeared.

Within these four walls,
I felt all the blame,
The guilt, the shame,
Echoing your name.

I began to see,
It was all my fault,
My strength locked away,
Inside of your vault.

I took all the blame,
Carried the weight,
Believing it was me
Who sealed our fate.

I thought it was love,
That turned into hate,
But deep down inside,
I was sealed in your gate.

12. Rooms In My Head

It happened again,
This time much worse,
In our bed,
Under your curse.

Each room in my mind,
A shadow of pain,
The walls were smeared,
With my endless disdain.

My greatest fears,
All coming true,
The horror of it all,
Of monsters like you.

13. Markers

We moved house,
Again and again,
So no one would see,
All of my pain.

Each time that I called,
I'd silence my tone,
Our addresses marked,
So I wasn't alone.

Each time they arrived,
I'd beg them to leave,
The fear in your eyes,
I couldn't believe.

My love, so afraid,
Desperate, in need,
This love was mine,
My job to retrieve.

14. I Do

I wanted to be worthy,
Of a man like you,
Who got all the girls,
And took what he wanted too.

We picked out a ring,
And of course, I said yes,
I dreamed of forever,
In a white dress.

Finally,
You saw my worth,
I thought this meant
It couldn't get worse.

A bouquet of bruises,
With each hymn's verse,
But it didn't matter,
I was your universe.

I was the one,
You chose from them all,
To carry your name,
To rise and to fall.

15. Death Do Us Part

Till death do us part,
That's what we swore,
In all of our homes,
Cuddled up, wanting more.

That image of you,
I once held so dear,
Until one day,
You became my fear.

I looked in the mirror,
Skin and bone,
Most nights awake,
Chilled and alone.

The thought of you,
Made me sick to the core,
It hit me at once,
Like a slam on the floor.

Suddenly I saw,
All that you'd done,
I had to leave,
To survive, to run.

16. Caged Bird

I packed up my bags,
Heard the birds sing,
Hopeful and bright,
For what the future would bring.

A future from afar,
Far from those shades of blue,
I cradled my babies,
And we ran from you.

We deserved better,
But you had no clue,
Your babies,
Were so scared of you.

Our home, our prison,
Not much longer,
This caged bird
Was growing much stronger.

The moving van booked,
A new home in sight,
Where people like you
Would never take flight.

A secret so safe,
Far from your spell,
A life that was ours,
Away from this hell.

17. Home Sweet Home

We made it so far,
Found a safe space,
A comfy new bed,
In our peaceful place.

A home of our own,
Far from the vile,
This secret of mine,
Worth every trial.

The first home we had,
In so long a time,
Out of the darkness,
We'd slowly climb.

Step by step,
Little by little,
With hope on my side,
A case for acquittal.

Walls once tarnished,
Now fresh and bright,
Clear of the evil,
And out of your sight.

18. The Journey

Far from you,
Away from your prison,
But inside my head,
Those memories risen.

Reminders of weakness,
A love never given,
A journey that lasts,
I must stay driven.

No matter the day,
You're never forgiven,
A lesson I learned,
A chance I was given.

One step at a time,
I'll learn to walk free,
A life without running,
A life meant for me.

A new way of thinking,
The damage you did,
It fades in the light,
A strength I once hid.

19. A Woman Was Born

A heart still big,
Full of hope each day,
But I'm afraid to say,
My love comes with a price to pay.

I no longer trust,
The words that I hear,
For it was words that broke me,
And filled me with fear.

I speak my truth,
I'm self-aware,
But that truth,
It often lays me bare.

A young girl died,
And a woman was born,
I wear my scars proudly,
For in them, I've sworn.

For this is what made me,
The woman you see,
I owe it to myself,
To grow and be free.

To find a man worthy,
Of standing by me,
To share in the strength,
That I've come to be.

20. Little Pink Pills

These little pink pills,
So hard to swallow,
Demons inside me,
I refuse to follow.

Down a dark path,
Of sadness and pain,
I won't let those thoughts
Take control again.

In my mind,
I keep them at bay,
Not letting them near,
I push them away.

Triggers of the past,
They scare me each day,
It's not what I wanted,
But these pills lead the way.

These little pink pills,
Though hard to take,
They help me feel numb,
They make my smiles seem fake.

21. After Life

I remind myself daily,
Of all that I am,
I am good and kind,
And if I keep trying,
I know that I can.

Quitting's not an option,
I refuse to stand still,
A new mindset born,
With strength and will.

I've got things to do,
A new life to create,
I've got so much to give,
No time to hesitate.

I have people who love me,
Wherever I go,
People who need me,
This time it's real,

not for show.

I'm proud of myself,
For standing right here,
This is my wealth,
My heart, my strength, my cheer.

www.ingramcontent.com/pod-product-compliance
Lightning Source LLC
Chambersburg PA
CBHW051743130826
49812CB00033B/987
* 9 7 8 9 3 7 0 9 2 2 2 1 1 *